Contents

Speaking Up

Greta Thunberg was only 16 years old.

But she was talking to world leaders.

She told them about **climate change**.

BEARCUB BIOS

GRETA THUNBERG

TEEN CLIMATE ACTIVIST

by Rachel Rose

Consultant: Beth Gambro
Reading Specialist, Yorkville, Illinois

BEARPORT PUBLISHING

Minneapolis, Minnesota

Teaching Tips

BEFORE READING

- Discuss what a biography is. What kinds of things might a biography tell a reader?
- Look through the glossary together. Read and discuss the words.
- Go on a picture walk, looking through the pictures to discuss vocabulary and make predictions about the text.

DURING READING

- Encourage readers to point to each word as it is read. Stop occasionally to ask readers to point to a specific word in the text.
- If a reader encounters an unknown word, ask them to look at the rest of the page. Are there any clues to help them understand?

AFTER READING

- Check for understanding.
  - Where was Greta Thunberg born?
  - What does she do?
  - What does she care about?
- Ask the readers to think deeper.
  - If you met Greta, what question would you like to ask her? Why?

Credits:
Cover and title page, © Daniele COSSU/Shutterstock; 3, © photocosmos1/Shutterstock; 5, © FABRICE COFFRINI/Getty Images; 7, © Nikolay Antonov/Shutterstock; 8-9, © FloridaStock/Shutterstock; 11, © STEFAN WERMUTH/Getty Images; 13, © FILIPPO MONTEFORTE/Getty Images; 14-15, © Sheila Fitzgerald/Shutterstock; 16-17, © JOHANNES EISELE/Getty Images; 19T, © ATTILA KISBENEDEK/Getty Images; 19B, © Ryan Remiorz/The Canadian Press via AP; 21, © Daniele COSSU/Shutterstock; 22, © Antonello Marangi/Shutterstock; 23TL, © New Africa/Shutterstock; 23TR, © SeppFriedhuber/iStock; 23BL, © Win McNamee/Getty Images; and 23BR, © Halfpoint/Shutterstock.

Library of Congress Cataloging-in-Publication Data

Names: Rose, Rachel, 1968– author. Title: Greta Thunberg : teen climate activist / by Rachel Rose. Description: Bearcub books. | Minneapolis : Bearport Publishing Company, 2020. | Series: Bearcub bios | Includes bibliographical references and index. Identifiers: LCCN 2019059832 | ISBN 9781642809770 (library binding) | ISBN 9781642809886 (paperback) | ISBN 9781642809992 (ebook) Subjects: LCSH: Thunberg, Greta, 2003—Juvenile literature. | Child environmentalists—Sweden—Biography—Juvenile literature. | Environmentalists—Sweden—Biography—Juvenile literature. Classification: LCC GE56.T58 R67 2020 | DDC 363.738/74092 [B]—dc23 LC record available at https://lccn.loc.gov/2019059832

For more information, write to Bearport Publishing, 5357 Penn Avenue South, Minneapolis, MN 55419.

Printed in the United States of America.

WORLD
ECONOMIC
FORUM
THUNBERG
HAL

Greta's Life

Greta was born in Sweden.

When she was young, she learned about climate change.

She learned that Earth is getting too hot.

The city where Greta was born

Greta learned there are **flooding** waters.

There are big storms.

Animals are dying.

She wanted to help.

Greta wanted many people to know about the problem.

So, she went on **strike**.

She stopped going to school.

This says "school strike for climate."

Many people heard about Greta.

Soon, others joined her.

Kids around the world wanted to help, too.

RESPECT YOUR MOTHER
LOVE NATURE AND RELAX
SAVE

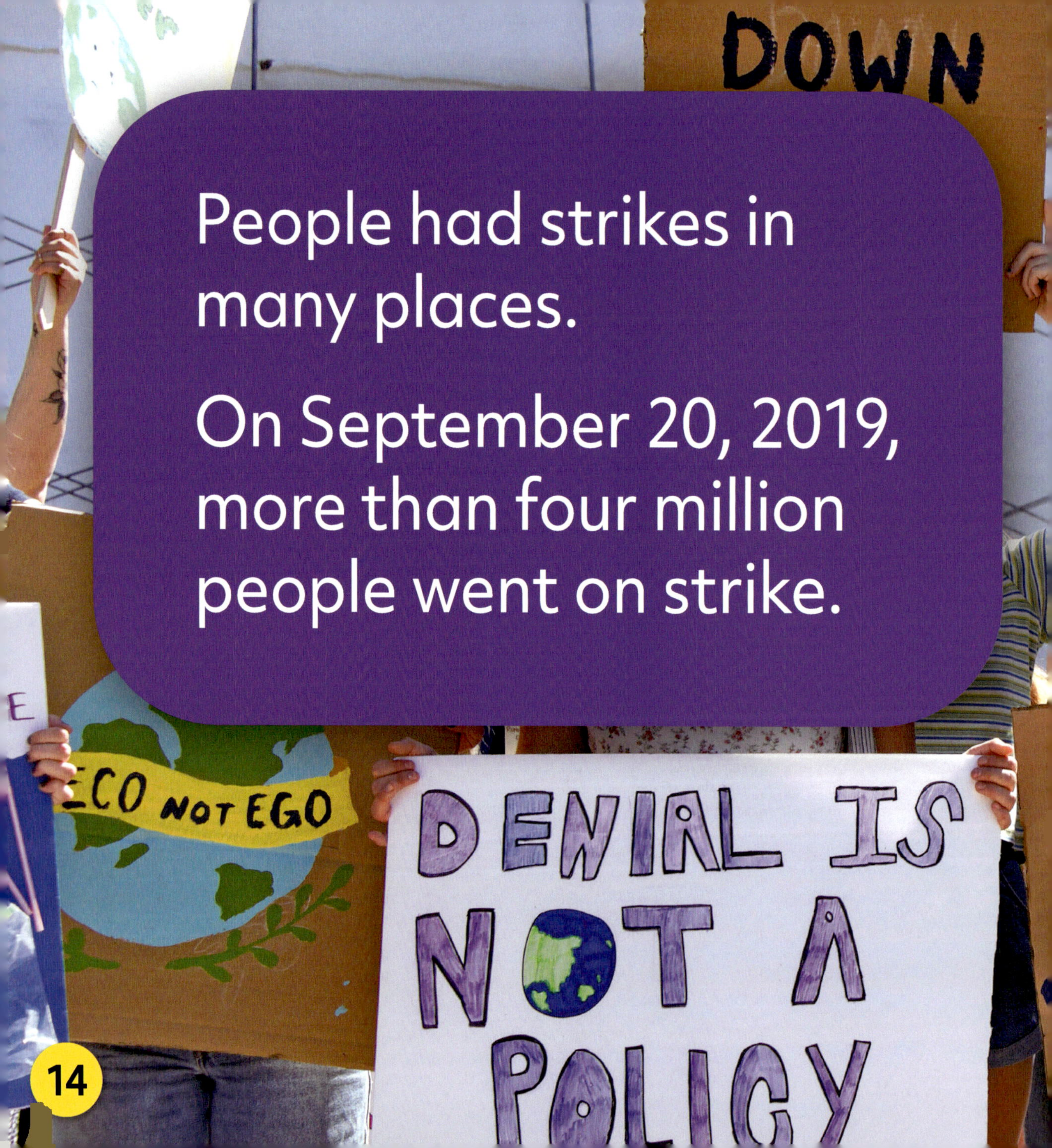

People had strikes in many places.

On September 20, 2019, more than four million people went on strike.

generation
OUR
CHOICE
GREEN ENERGY
CREATES
JOBS TOO!
our
Climate
is changing...
WHY AREN'T
THE
CHANGING
SYSTEM
CHANGE
NOT
CLIMATE
CHANGE

Greta joined strikes in New York.

She traveled there by boat and not by plane.

Planes are not good for Earth.

Malizia
Global Climate Action
United Nations Climate Change

Greta has worked hard to help Earth.

She has talked with many people.

Presidents and world leaders have heard her.

President Obama

Prime Minister Trudeau

Greta has made a difference.

Helping Earth is the most important thing to Greta.

She wants it to be important to everyone.

CLIMA

Did You Know?

Born: January 3, 2003

Family: Malena (mother), Svante (father), Beata (sister)

When she was a kid: Doctors told her she had a kind of **autism**. Greta says this gives her a superpower.

Special fact: Greta was named *Time*'s Person of the Year in 2019.

Greta says: "When I grow up, I want to be able to look back and say that I did everything I could."

Life Connections

Greta thinks there is a lot people can do to make Earth better. Is there something you can do to make the world better?

Glossary

autism something that can make it hard to communicate or be with other people

climate change the warming of Earth's air and oceans

flooding huge amounts of water spreading over land

strike to stop doing something in order to make a change

Index

Read More

Chancellor, Deborah. *Save the Animals (Good to Be Green).* New York: Crabtree Publishing (2020).

Lawrence, Ellen. *Global Warming (Green World, Clean World).* New York: Bearport (2014).

Learn More Online

1. Go to **www.factsurfer.com**
2. Enter "**Greta Thunberg**" into the search box.
3. Click on the cover of this book to see a list of websites.

About the Author

Rachel Rose lives in San Francisco. Like many, she is inspired by Greta Thunberg. She wants to help make Earth a safer place.